JOHANNESBURG

THE CITY AT A GLANCE

Marble Towers
This 1973 striated glass-and-steel high-rise once had Africa's largest electronic sign but it blew off in a storm, never to be replaced.
208-212 Jeppe Street

Sun Hotel
Hotel magnate Sol Kerzner's late-1980s blue-glass folly (said to be inspired by the opening credits of *Dallas*) sits forlorn and empty, its lustre never to be repeated, unlike the show.
Jeppe Street/Von Wielligh Street

Ellis Park Stadium
South Africa's famous rugby arena dates to 1928. The modern version opened in 1982; the Springboks won the World Cup here in 1995.
See p088

Sentech Tower
Located in rough-and-tumble Brixton, this 1962 telecoms tower soars to nearly 235m.
Symons Road

Johannesburg Athletics Stadium
Designed by Arup and RFB, the 1995 bowl forms a distinctive crater in the city centre due to its 200m-long crescent-shaped roof.
124 Van Beek Street, T 011 407 8644

Ponte City
The smartest property in town in 1975 fell on hard times in the 1990s. But with investment finally forthcoming, Ponte City's 54 floors are set to define skyscraper living once again.
See p066

Hillbrow Tower
Joburg's other telecoms tower, completed in 1971, was a major draw until security concerns forced the closure of its observation deck.
See p012

INTRODUCTION

THE CHANGING FACE OF THE URBAN SCENE

Despite Johannesburg's brief history (it was only officially declared a city in 1928), it has seen more than its fair share of drama. It can also be confounding – traditional marketplaces meet sterile malls, finance guys live on farms, and corruption is common, although major projects like the mass-transit Gautrain arrive on time (if not on budget). South Africa's economic powerhouse was never considered a tourist destination until the 2010 FIFA World Cup, when it finally got to show off its fun side. Add to this Joburg's key role in the struggle against apartheid, its remarkable transition 20 years into democracy, and the fact that it was Nelson Mandela's home, and you have a city firmly on the global map.

The one-time mining town is now creating a different kind of gold through financial services, real estate, manufacturing and retail. You see it in the high-rises of Sandton, the cosmopolitan suburbs of Rosebank and Melrose Arch, and the thriving inner-city hubs of Newtown, Maboneng and Braamfontein, where creatives have transformed the landscape. It's not all shiny – the city is still playing catch-up after a century of segregation, which has left a legacy of disparate, spread-out districts, splintered infrastructure, and a conspicuous inequality. Yet, with a pan-cultural mix driving booming culinary, art and fashion scenes, it is entering a more refined phase. And as the country's most African city, it offers an intoxicating and often cacophonous injection of colour and style.

ESSENTIAL INFO

FACTS, FIGURES AND USEFUL ADDRESSES

TOURIST OFFICE
195 Jan Smuts Avenue
T 011 214 0700
www.joburgtourism.com

TRANSPORT
Airport transfer to city centre
Gautrains depart from 5am to 9pm. The journey (via Sandton) takes 25 minutes
www.gautrain.co.za
Car hire
Hertz
T 011 390 9700
Taxi
Maxi Taxi
T 011 648 1258
It's not safe to hail cabs on the street
Travel card
A Gautrain Gold Card costs R12 and can be topped up at stations as required

EMERGENCY SERVICES
Ambulance
T 10177
Fire/Police
T 10111
24-hour pharmacy
Netcare Linksfield Hospital
24 12th Avenue
T 011 647 3600

CONSULATES
British High Commission
255 Hill Street
Pretoria
T 012 421 7500
www.gov.uk/government/world/south-africa
US Consulate General
1 Sandton Drive
T 011 290 3000
southafrica.usembassy.gov

POSTAL SERVICES
Post office
Jeppe Street/Small Street
T 011 336 1361
www.postoffice.co.za
Shipping
UPS
Unit C, Brussels Road
T 011 922 9200

BOOKS
The Joburg Book edited by Nechama Brodie (Pan Macmillan/Sharp Sharp Media)
Johannesburg Transition: Architecture & Society From 1950 by Clive M Chipkin (STE Publishers)

WEBSITES
Architecture
www.artefacts.co.za
www.gifa.org.za
Arts/Culture
www.gauteng.net
Newspaper
www.timeslive.co.za

EVENTS
Arts Alive
www.artsalive.co.za

COST OF LIVING
Taxi from OR Tambo International Airport to Sandton
R350
Cappuccino
R20
Packet of cigarettes
R35
Daily newspaper
R3
Bottle of champagne
R800

JOHANNESBURG

Population
4.4 million

Currency
Rand

Telephone codes
South Africa: 27
Johannesburg: 011

Local time
GMT +2

Flight time
London: 11 hours

AVERAGE TEMPERATURE / °C

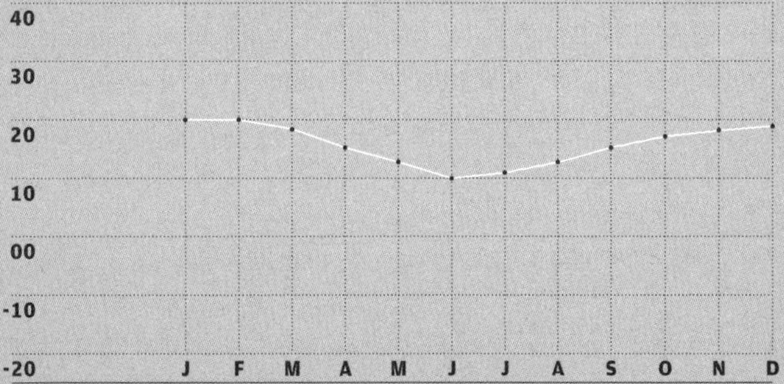

AVERAGE RAINFALL / MM

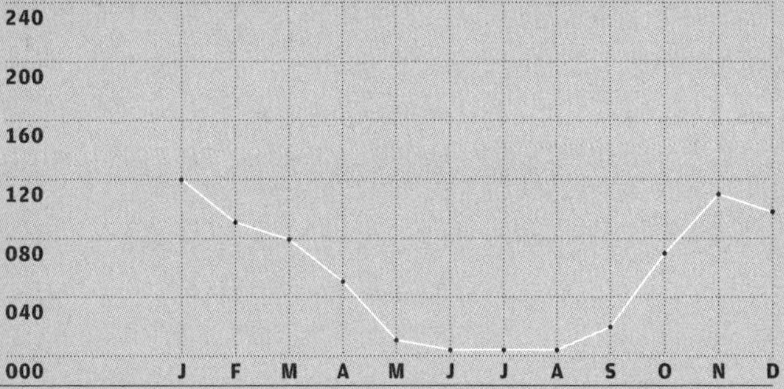

NEIGHBOURHOODS

THE AREAS YOU NEED TO KNOW AND WHY

To help you navigate the city, we've chosen the most interesting districts (see below and the map inside the back cover) and colour-coded our featured venues, according to their location; those venues that are outside these areas are not coloured.

SANDTON

Africa's swankiest enclave is home to chain hotels, premier shopping malls and Nelson Mandela Square (Rivonia Road/5th Street, T 011 217 6001). Here, the elite combine business and pleasure. Gleaming high-rise HQs of the continent's richest companies vie for attention near the Stock Exchange, and by late afternoon the ties have been loosened as moneymen fill up the swish restaurants, hotel lounges and pool bars.

MELROSE

Post-apartheid, the Melrose Arch precinct was planned as a modern multipurpose zone. Although its exclusivity, and relative blandness, is often sniffed at, it's a thriving alternative to the enclosed estates of the northern suburbs and a popular place for first-time visitors to stay. On the doorstep are chic hotels, cosmopolitan restaurants like Orient (see p057), and fine designer garments at Suzaan Heyns (see p084).

BRAAMFONTEIN/NEWTOWN

Connected by Nelson Mandela Bridge, this is Johannesburg's cultural heart. Creative types and developers have colonised Braamfontein, converting old warehouses and 1950s offices into design showrooms, galleries and nightspots. Newtown boasts Museum Africa (121 Bree Street, T 011 833 5624) and the city's hippest graffiti and street art, as well as a major shopping and office complex, Newtown Junction, that incorporates the historic Potato Sheds.

MABONENG/CBD

The CBD, location of the densest cluster of tower blocks in Africa (see p013), is on the rise again. Go for a walk down Main Street past Edwardian, art deco and modernist architecture, old mining houses and relics of the city's prospecting past, and have a drink in the posh Rand Club (33 Loveday Street, T 011 870 4260). Further east is Maboneng, where reclaimed industrial spaces have been turned into a network of contemporary live, work and play areas.

THE PARKS

A collection of leafy neighbourhoods, The Parks is residential but with a genuinely urban feel. It includes Parkhurst, where the 4th Avenue artery is lined with fashion stores, modern decor shops and cafés. In Parktown North, you'll find a row of art galleries (see p035) on Jan Smuts Avenue, and 7th Avenue has a range of good dining options. Parkview's village-like high street offers respite from the city's mall culture.

MELVILLE

Bobo Melville has vibrant street life and a strong community feel thanks to affordable rents in Victorian stock, and hip hangouts, such as vintage store Reminiscence (7th Street, T 011 726 7905), that lure students from the nearby universities. Dine out at the Italian restaurant La Luna (see p050) and head to Melville Koppies (Judith Road, T 011 482 4797) to view the veld and get a sense of how Joburg looked 125 years ago.

LANDMARKS

THE SHAPE OF THE CITY SKYLINE

Over an intense, chaotic century and a quarter, Joburg has adopted, rejected, demolished and all but replaced almost every popular design form of the times in a pervading culture of quick profit that continues to this day. Architect and author Clive Chipkin labelled the city's 'rentier architecture' as a 'dustbin of discarded styles'.

Relics of Johannesburg's gold-mining past can be found in the remaining headgear towers (there's one on pedestrianised Main Street in the CBD) and, south of the city, in the towering earthen mounds of industrial refuse. In the 1930s, Joburg was known as the 'Manhattan of the veld' for its art deco buildings – one of the best examples is the restored Barbican (Loveday Street/President Street) – and, briefly, was considered to be a focal point of the modernism promoted by Le Corbusier, until the next fad took over.

The signature skyline dates from the ambitious architectural commissions of the 1960s and 1970s, bookended by Sentech Tower (Symons Road) and Ponte City (see p066), with Hillbrow Tower (see p012) and Carlton Centre (see p013) in-between, along with the 284m Nelson Mandela Bridge, which, since 2003, has linked Braamfontein with Newtown across 42 railway lines. However, high-rises are now sprouting in Sandton, where decentralisation and new transport hubs have resulted in a crop of distinctive (if not always attractive) monuments to financial clout (overleaf).

For full addresses, see Resources.

Alexander Forbes Building

The eight-storey HQ of financial services firm Alexander Forbes occupies 100,000 sq m opposite Sandton Gautrain station. Designed by Paragon, its eco-friendly bulk sits on concrete columns protected by a concrete-bracket roof that provides deep overhang. Big grey 'scallop' wings scoop light into the back of the building; horizontal louvres on the glass-fronted Rivonia Road side curb its penetration. Inside, vast atriums display a landscaped environment filled with 6m-high weeping figs, reflecting ponds, and veneers and cladding in natural materials. As well as offices, there's a beauty salon, a crèche, a gym, prayer rooms and preferential parking for pool cars and hybrid models. It marks a trend for greener building in Johannesburg's new business precincts.
115 West Street, T 011 269 0000

Hillbrow Tower

One of the most recognisable landmarks in the city, Hillbrow Tower (officially known as the Telkom Tower) is now an enduring symbol of Johannesburg's 20th-century vigour. Named after the suburb in which it is located, the communications hub was constructed over three years and gave the skyline a futuristic, cosmopolitan visage upon its completion in 1971. Including the spire of its antenna, it rises to 270m, while its sturdy walls reach 84cm thick. A structure of such prominence was an obvious spot for a revolving restaurant and observation deck – both were once found on its six public floors, which closed in the early 1980s. Back then, Hillbrow Tower was the biggest tourist lure in town. Today, its locale is a contested transitional urban zone, better viewed with a guide.
Goldreich Street/Banket Street

Carlton Centre

For more than 40 years, the Carlton Centre has been the tallest occupied building in Africa: a 50-storey, 223m concrete slab opened in 1973. Designed by Skidmore, Owings & Merrill, it is a towering legacy to the ambitions of the apartheid regime. The neighbouring upside-down Y-shaped Carlton Hotel was the site of key events in the shift to democratic rule, including the 1991 Peace Accord signing. Crime and decentralisation saw the complex lose its lustre and, by the early 1990s, much of it was vacant; the hotel closed in 1997. The Carlton Centre was subsequently bought by freight firm Transnet, and, due to the turnaround of the CBD, now operates at nearly full occupancy, offering a bustling retail arcade at the base and a viewing deck – the Top of Africa – at the summit.
150 Commissioner Street, T 011 308 1331

A. MOOSA BLANKETS

11 Diagonal Street

Completed in 1984, 11 Diagonal is one of the last major modernist undertakings of the apartheid era, a 32,600 sq m office tower that was designed by Helmut Jahn in collaboration with architects Louis Karol. Situated in what was Joburg's first financial quarter, it is surrounded by a clutch of original structures from the early 1900s, including the WH Stucke-designed Rosenberg Building (10 Diagonal Street), and the area's traditional *muti* (medicine) stores (see p030). The facade – a very 1980s curtain of reflective glass supported by a concrete-and-steel framework – was designed to evoke a diamond, in a nod to the mineral resources that made the city rich. The opulence persists inside, where a five-storey atrium is finished in the same mirrored glass as the exterior. And now that deep-pocketed bank Absa is its owner, the building should continue to shine.
11 Diagonal Street

HOTELS

WHERE TO STAY AND WHICH ROOMS TO BOOK

Johannesburg was reborn as a tourist destination with the success of the 2010 FIFA World Cup, and visitor numbers have been on the up since, as the city gradually sheds its reputation as a dangerous place to visit. It is still playing catch up with Cape Town in terms of contemporary interior design but a growing number of residential properties have been converted into stylish boutique options and global brands are moving in – the Four Seasons arrived in 2014 with an overhaul of the iconic Westcliff (67 Jan Smuts Avenue, T 011 481 6000), adding a mod-African aesthetic and a destination spa.

In the northern suburbs, AtholPlace (90 Pretoria Avenue, T 011 783 3410), which has chic urban-rustic decor, The Peech (opposite) and Ten Bompas (see p036) evoke a vaguely Bel-Air-below-the-equator feel. In Rosebank, the refit of a post office into the Monarch (167 Oxford Road, T 011 341 2000) portended the trend towards sensitive restoration. Nearby, The Winston (6 Tottenham Avenue, T 011 268 3140) resembles an English manor house, set around a lovely pool. The stately InterContinental (Maude Street/5th Street, T 011 780 5555), Radisson Blu Gautrain (Rivonia Road, T 011 286 1000) and The Maslow (146 Rivonia Road, T 010 226 4600) offer excellent dining in the heart of the city's business hub. And for quirky inner-city living, there's stylish budget hotel The Bannister (9 De Beer Street, T 011 403 6888) and arty 12 Decades (see p021). *For full addresses and room rates, see Resources.*

The Peech

This smart suburban hideaway exemplifies Joburg's current boutique trend. The 1950s duplex apartment complex was converted by architect Kate Otten into a well-priced, well-located hotel set in lush gardens with an outdoor pool. The 16 understated but large rooms are stylishly decorated with African furnishings like Ngumi cowhide rugs, graphic 'Wabi Sabi' wallpaper and sculptures from Amatuli Artefacts. Those farthest from the pool, such as the Garden Suite (Room 16, above), are the quietest. The bistro serves an international menu, as well as a complimentary breakfast of wraps and smoothies, and makes good use of ingredients from its own kitchen garden. There's no gym on site, but a public fitness centre is just next door.
61 North Street, T 011 537 9797, www.thepeech.co.za

The Satyagraha House

This guesthouse/museum, once home to Mahatma Gandhi, was designed by his friend Hermann Kallenbach, and the two lived here in 1908 and 1909. It is inspired by a traditional *kraal* (farmhouse; opposite) with two *rondavels* (thatched-roof circular huts), in which Gandhi's life is captured in photos, possessions and letters, and his teachings etched in wood – it was here he developed the philosophy of Satyagraha (non-violent resistance). Seven rooms are spread between the main house, a cottage and a 2010 wing (Henri Polak Superior Room, above) added by Rocco Bosman, and contain furniture, fabrics and antiques from Gujarat, Gandhi's home state. There is wi-fi but no TV – instead devour the philosophical texts in the reading room.
15 Pine Road, T 011 485 5928, www.satyagrahahouse.com

The Hamilton

Designed by architects StudioMAS, who gave us CIRCA (see p035), and opened in 2010 on a residential street close to Rosebank and Hyde Park, The Hamilton blends into its surroundings, the natural tones of its concrete facade and green glass in harmony with the leafy northern suburbs. Local firm Mezzanine designed the interiors with contrasting rough and smooth surfaces in monochrome accented with zingy chartreuse, and photographs and prints by South African artists. Six compact rooms overlook the plunge pool (above) and landscaped walled garden; a corrugated roof overhang references the old Johannesburg houses. Split-level Suite 4, which has a freestanding bath in the square bay window, is the most coveted. *28 Grosvenor Avenue, T 011 447 9280, www.thehamilton.co.za*

12 Decades

Atop a residential block in Maboneng, this art hotel showcases the city's history in 12 rooms, each conceived by a local designer. Our favourites are the Bauhaus- and De Stijl-inspired Minehaus (1916-1926) by Dokter and Misses (see p026); A Part Love A Part Hate (1946-1956), a statement on apartheid laws by Bradley Kirshenbaum of Love Jozi (see p078); and Catwalk Customs (1986-1996), a homage to vogueing by Black Coffee (see p078). The hotel is self-service but there's a rooftop boxing gym, and the lobby (above) on the ground floor doubles as a gallery. You're also on the doorstep of such varied dining spots as Little Addis (see p024), The Blackanese (see p040) and Canteen (see p054).
Main Street Life Building,
286 Fox Street, T 011 026 5601,
www.urbanhiphotels.com/12-decades

African Pride Melrose Arch Hotel

Melrose Arch may seem soulless at times but it pioneered the live, work and play concept – a walkable, secure district that comprises offices, restaurants, shops and luxury flats – that is being emulated on a less-grand scale in Maboneng. Although the decor in this 2003 hotel verges on the kitsch, it has much to offer and service is top-notch. Architect Guy Steenekamp and designer Les Harbottle created 118 spacious rooms (Superior, above) with big bathrooms. Quirks include rubber ducks in baths, oversized planters, and an entrance walkway that lights up like a red carpet. The clubby Library Bar is a hive of deals, while the garden area, including cabanas, a maze and a pool with tables and chairs in the shallow end, is a fine place to unwind.
1 Melrose Square, T 011 214 6666, www.africanpridehotels.com

Saxon Hotel, Villas and Spa

Sandhurst is home to the monied set, and the pricey and chic Saxon illustrates this affluence. Everything about this 53-suite property, converted by Ridler Shepherd Low, is huge. Rooms begin at about 80 sq m, and are done out with African antiques and sizeable marble baths. The Executive Luxury Suites found in the 2010 extension feature light wood and stone cladding, and access to a pool and terrace. On the lower levels of the original building, rooms, such as the Luxury One Bedroom (above), open on to landscaped gardens. The halls are (discreetly) adorned with portraits of guests such as Mandela, who worked on *Long Walk to Freedom* here. The spa (see p089) is an institution and Five Hundred is one of the best restaurants in South Africa.
36 Saxon Road, T 011 292 6000, www.saxon.co.za

24 HOURS

SEE THE BEST OF THE CITY IN JUST ONE DAY

Joburg's reputation as an in-and-out kinda town, a safari-goers' pitstop, is shifting. The business capital of Africa has much to offer aside from its ubiquitous malls. Around the CBD, hip design and retail hubs like Braamfontein and Maboneng (see p031) sit beside medicine markets (see p030) and the excellent coffee and food of the Ethiopian Quarter ('Little Addis') – head for the Medical Arts Building (220 Jeppe Street). The Fashion Kapitol (130 Pritchard Street, T 011 333 7372) is also a must-visit for its street style and local *shweshwe* fabrics. These areas are best seen with a guide.

Given the city's size, it's easiest to travel by car (or use a pick-up app service like Uber), but you can now take the Gautrain, or rapid-transit Rea Vaya buses. There's too much to squeeze into a day but if you're disciplined you could spend the morning in culture hubs such as WAM (see p028) and CIRCA (see p034), and the afternoon in Soweto (see p032), so integral to the anti-apartheid movement, where Mandela House (8115 Vilakazi Street, T 011 936 7754) vies with quad-bike excursions to backstreet taverns (*shebeens*), led by Soweto Outdoor Adventures (Dynamo Street, T 072 692 8159).

For dinner, secure a table at The Leopard (see p037) on the doorstep of Melville's 7th Street, lined with happening bars. Or head to Thomas Maxwell (see p051) and then nearby cocktail bar Cocoon (24 Central, Fredman Drive/Gwen Lane, T 011 783 2316).

For full addresses, see Resources.

08.30 The Whippet in Linden

Set in the old Linden Hotel in the heart of the former 'posh' Afrikaaner suburb, The Whippet serves a contemporary helping of traditional hospitality. Lace doilies have been ditched for slick design referencing the district's heritage, incorporating face brick, concrete floors, recycled tables and a church pew, as well as shelving by local company Woodlady. The lights are made from peach jars – in the early 1930s, farms here were the main exporter of peaches to the UK. Tuck into the house breakfast featuring a perfect tempura poached egg or classic sweet treats such as the creamy *melktert* (milk tart dusted with cinnamon). It's also a great spot for lunch due to the natural light that streams through floor-to-ceiling windows. Closed Sundays.
4th Avenue/7th Street, T 011 782 7310, www.thewhippetcoffee.com

10.00 Dokter and Misses

Husband-and-wife team Adriaan Hugo and Katy Taplin's bold, quirky furniture, cabinets, mirrors and lighting are highly covetable – the pieces, which decorate some of the hippest interiors in town, appear to possess an innate energy. The store also carries clever outdoor items by Joe Paine. Stroll-friendly Juta Street is a fine mix of galleries, cafés and eateries.
68 Juta Street, T 011 403 1024

10.30 Wits Art Museum

Architects Nina Cohen and Fiona Garson masterfully transformed a former garage forecourt and basement into a new home for WAM in 2012. This is no white box: a swathe of brickwork in a basket-weave pattern wraps around the building above enormous panes of glass that front 5,000 sq m of space, while interesting curves and sightlines are provided by ramps, pillars and double-height skylights. There are more than 9,000 pieces in the collection, which includes historical artefacts as well as contemporary South African art – look out for Jackson Hlungwani's *Women's Altar to God*, Willem Boshoff's *The Purple Shall Govern* and Robert Hodgins' *A Beast Slouches* – and works from Western and Central Africa. There's a busy café here too.
University Corner, Bertha Street/Jorissen Street, T 011 717 1365, www.wits.ac.za

12.00 Museum of Man & Science

Devoted to the art of traditional African medicine, *muti* shops abound in the old downtown close to Diagonal Street, the city's first financial district, and the Mai Mai and Faraday Markets. Set among a throng of mobile-phone sellers and fabric stores, Man & Science is a museum in the sense that it displays historic artefacts. As for the science, there's plenty of that too, thanks to its dried monkey carcass, jars of crushed herbs and vials of coloured powders and animal hair, its ceiling a mass of dried grasses, bones and beadwork. The shop might be a curiosity for visitors, but it remains a working practice, attracting *sangomas* (spiritual healers) and *inyangas* (herbalists), who use such items not only to heal the sick but to counteract curses cast by jealous rivals and spurned lovers. *14 Diagonal Street, T 011 836 4470*

12.45 Maboneng Precinct

Property developer Jonathan Liebmann has masterminded the transformation of a swathe of inner-city blocks into a thriving lifestyle playground. At its heart is Arts on Main (see p054), which kickstarted the regeneration in 2009, and, since 2013, the Museum of African Design (T 011 592 0517), which is located in a cavernous red-brick hall with art deco elements. Curator Aaron Kohn says its mission is to become a pan-continental cultural hub with a wide-ranging remit to cater for disciplines such as fashion, as well as hosting exhibitions. Maboneng has steadily built an inspiring collection of street art, including large-scale pieces such as Steve 'ESPO' Powers' *Mama Afrika* (above) on Artisan Lofts (264 Market Street). Mainstreetwalks (T 072 880 9583) offers guided tours of the area. *www.mabonengprecinct.com*

14.30 Soweto

Taking its name from the designation South Western Township, Soweto contains roughly a third of Joburg's population. It's something of a schlep from the centre, and you could easily spend a day exploring sights like the Hector Pieterson Museum (T 011 536 0611) in Orlando West – an austere structure by architects MRA that commemorates the uprising of 1976. Also worth a look is the 2012 Lego-like Soweto Theatre (T 011 930 7461), near Jabulani station. Designed by Afritects, the vibrant ceramic-tiled red, yellow and blue theatres are backed by two black parabolic blocks. Alternatively, make your way to Orlando Towers (pictured; T 071 674 4343), a pair of 100m-high cooling towers, constructed in 1951 on Dynamo Street. In 2008, they were transformed into an adventure sports zone, complete with abseiling, bungee jumping, climbing and more. The murals took six months to finish.

Cool
First National
How

16.30 **Goodman Gallery and CIRCA**

Jan Smuts Avenue is home to some of the city's top art spaces. The Goodman Gallery shows a core of blue-chip South African artists including William Kentridge, and photographers Kudzanai Chiurai, David Goldblatt and Mikhael Subotzky ('Two Projects', above). Over the road, browse the books, prints and art at Maker (T 011 447 6680) and David Krut Projects (see p085). On the corner of Jellicoe Avenue is CIRCA, a solar-powered oval-shaped building – distinctively clad in a scrim of slim, vertical aluminium poles (opposite) by StudioMAS' Pierre Swanepoel – that displays large installations. Behind here is the oldest commercial gallery in Africa, Everard Read (T 011 788 4805), which features a distinguished roster.

163 Jan Smuts Avenue, T 011 788 1113; 2 Jellicoe Avenue, T 011 788 4805

19.00 **The Winehouse**

A portrait of Amy Winehouse, by artist Joanna Flatau, gave this bar/restaurant its name. It has the feel of a chic bistro due to its banquettes, muted palette and menu of French staples prepared by Dominik Middlecamp and Andrew Scott Fleet. A glass-fronted, double-volume wine cellar, housing a vast collection of South African vintages, overlooks the garden terrace and sleek pool, which is a lovely spot for a pre-dinner drink – sample one of the Cape labels from Stellenbosch or Elgin Valley. Winehouse is part of the 10-suite Ten Bompas, which opened in 1996 as the city's first true boutique hotel, designed by architect Luc Zeghers. It still lures a well-heeled clientele who like its central location and collection of African art.
Ten Bompas Hotel, 10 Bompas Road, T 011 341 0282, www.tenbompas.com

20.30 **The Leopard**

Chef Andrea Burgener has been a fixture on Joburg's food scene for more than 15 years. Her current domain, The Leopard, is a laidback operation but still it's almost impossible to get a table without booking well in advance. The adventurous menu incorporates African takes on classics like steak tartare, as well as Asian flavours and Middle Eastern ingredients – perhaps try the Mozambican piri-piri quail stuffed with macadamias and herbs, followed by halva, yogurt, roasted nuts, honey and rose syrup. The mismatched retro decor is thrown together with as much aplomb as the cuisine, featuring key pieces collected by Burgener over the years, notably the selection of 1960s to 1980s lights that hang from the artex ceiling.

63a 4th Avenue, T 011 482 9356,
www.leopardfoodcompany.com

22.30 Randlords

Perched 22 storeys up at the highest point in Braamfontein, Randlords – named after the city's first gold barons and designed to evoke a similar level of entitlement and prestige – has wraparound views from Soweto to Sandton. Lesley Carstens and Silvio Rech, better known for their safari lodges, have created an ultra-sleek urban lounge, with wooden floors and decking, mirrored ceilings, a bar topped by blown glass orbs, beaded swings, plush sofas and tree-trunk tables, yet the floor-to-ceiling glass ensures the primary feature is the city itself. An expansive terrace is furnished with daybeds and fire pits. The venue is often booked for events, so check online first. If it's closed, try Great Dane (T 011 403 1136) or Kitchener's Carvery Bar (see p062) for late-night revelry.

South Point Towers, 41 De Korte Street, T 011 489 1930, www.randlords.co.za

URBAN LIFE

CAFÉS, RESTAURANTS, BARS AND NIGHTCLUBS

After decades of Cape Town dominance in culinary innovation and sophistication, Joburg is hitting back. In 2013, Five Hundred (see p023) was the runner-up in the country's most prestigious restaurant awards and DW Eleven-13 (Shop 11-13, Dunkeld West, T 011 341 0663) also scored highly. The city cannot be bettered in terms of sheer choice. For Mozambican food, try Parreirinha (9 6th Street, La Rochelle, T 011 435 3809), set in a former police station; Ethiopian *injera* platters are served at Little Addis Cafe (180 Fox Street, T 082 683 8675); and sushi gets a makeover at The Blackanese (20 Kruger Street, T 011 024 9455) through biltong and curry flavours. Steakhouses have always been popular – two of the best are Turn 'n Tender (see p056) and The Grillhouse (Shop 70, The Firs, Oxford Road/Biermann Avenue, T 011 880 3945), but burgers washed down with craft beer is the new way to enjoy your meat. Try the retro-style Wolfpack (21 4th Avenue, T 011 447 7705).

Coffee is a religion here and Father (opposite), Croft & Co (see p042) and Warm & Glad (see p060) double as work spaces. For upscale drinks, sup poolside cocktails at The Maslow (see p016) or Radisson Blu (see p016). After-hours, check out Braamfontein, its once-dark alleyways spruced up with public art – head to Great Dane (see p038) or Kitchener's (see p062) – and Melville's 7th Street for quirky bars like Liberation Café (No 5a, T 011 026 6217). *For full addresses, see Resources.*

Father Coffee

The Scandi-style white-ash herringbone interiors of Father Coffee were intended to evoke the feeling of a warm cabin in a forest. Designed by the four owners, it is beautifully minimal, from the copper-piping light fixtures to the elegant cups commissioned from the Ceramic Factory (see p076) and the svelte, geometric logo. A limited menu features croissants and sweet treats on weekends, but the focus is on the beans – roasted in a 5kg Diedrich that takes pride of place. For more coffee culture nearby, Post (T 072 248 2078) is a haven for vinyl junkies, while Doubleshot Coffee and Tea (T 011 100 5241) has a reverence for the leaf. Some of the Father team are behind hip Asian-fusion bistro Good Luck Club (T 011 447 3816) in Illovo.
Shop 2, 73 Juta Street, T 082 513 4258, www.fathercoffee.co.za

ENTRANCE
THIS WAY!

Croft & Co

Located on the high street in Parkview, this coffeeshop has a neighbourhood vibe, all rustic wood, industrial finishes and a deep-etched concrete street-art portrait by Hannelie Coetzee. The menu is unembellished but still tempting, and the place is renowned for its creamy scrambled eggs, juices (try the spinach and kale) and *prego* (steak) rolls.
66 Tyrone Avenue, T 011 646 3634

STANLEY
ORDER HERE

Stanley Beer Yard

This is the ultimate boys' hangout. The eclectic interior falls somewhere between a Victorian curiosity shop, a Karoo country kitchen and a hunting lodge, complete with trophy heads and bell-jar dioramas, and a mismatched assortment of wooden tables and chairs in what resembles an industrial shed. There's a robust offering of local craft beers, such as Jack Black Butcher Block Pale Ale (smooth, US-style with a floral aroma) and Cape Brewing Company's Amber Weiss (fruity, dark, aromatic, German-style), and a small but excellent selection of South African wine. The upmarket pub grub goes big on meat including local sausages and charcuterie. Thursday nights and weekends often offer a mix of vinyl-spinning DJs, and there's live music on Saturday afternoons.
44 Stanley Avenue, T 011 482 5791

Assaggi

Set in a small shopping centre in Illovo, its white-clothed tables spilling out along the tiled walkways, Assaggi specialises in pared-down Italian food – the veal dishes are exceptional, as are the *zucchini fritti*, and signature asparagus and brie lasagne. Italian-born chef Fabrizio Mercuri took over from gregarious owner Luciana Righi, who brought a strong dose of the mother country with her when she arrived from Ravenna in the 1980s, but it still remains perennially packed, popular by day with the executive lunch crowd. Its seemingly humble surroundings are dispelled by one look at the gleaming rides in the car park. Bring along a local to help with people-spotting – Assaggi has become a haven for politicos, business bigwigs and socialites. *Post Office Centre, 30 Rudd Road, T 011 268 1370, www.assaggi.co.za*

Cube Tasting Kitchen

Chef Dario de Angeli burst on to the scene in 1999 with Yum in Greenside, which he ran for seven years, and critics predicted great things. He hasn't disappointed here. The suburban premises is essentially a white cube, decorated with just a Dokter and Misses 'Kreep' planter on the wall, to create a blank canvas that doesn't detract from the food. The seasonal menu presents fascinating juxtapositions of textures and tastes, such as shiitake mushroom with baked custard, vinegar gel and rosemary, and the presentation is beautiful. It's BYO, corkage is free and pairings are proposed in advance. A mere 30 covers are served each night and the ten-course (or more) meal (R575) unfolds over three to four hours – a rarity in fast-paced Joburg.
Shop 5, Parknorth Heights, 17 4th Avenue, T 082 422 8158, www.cubekitchen.co.za

The Great Eastern Food Bar

The Bamboo Centre is a dose of upmarket dining and retail in middle-class Melville. Alongside boutiques – such as Love Books (T 011 726 7408) and Black Coffee (see p078) – and a Saturday farmers' market, Service Station (T 011 726 1701) is popular for its pay-by-the-pound buffet brunch. Have lunch or dinner at the top-floor Great Eastern Food Bar, which has a lovely view over the Melville Koppies nature reserve. The interior makes use of raw brick, South African bleached pine and American ash, and the leafy potted garden that adorns the shutters supplies the place with some of its herbs. Chef Nick Scott's short, ever-changing Asian menu consists of dishes with delicate yet intense flavours, such as dumplings of kimchi and oriental greens.
Bamboo Centre, 53 Rustenberg Road/ 9th Street, T 011 482 2910

La Luna

Klaus Beckmann and pastry chef Lindy Pretorius both worked at the Westcliff Hotel, before it closed for conversion into the Four Seasons (see p016), and can be credited with raising the tone of Melville's 7th Street, previously better known for cut-price cocktails and funky nightspots (see p040). Due to its tranquil navy-and-cream interiors, reclaimed and African wood furniture by Michael van Olphen for FOSS, collection of retro mirrors and lovely patio, La Luna is more private yacht than party boat. The fine Italian fare includes signature dishes such as oxtail agnolotti, osso buco, and bayleaf panna cotta with lemon jelly and strawberries, making this one place where it's definitely worth your while saving space for dessert.

9 7th Street, T 011 482 7451,
www.laluna-melville.co.za

Thomas Maxwell

Concrete floors and exposed brick give this sceney bistro an NYC feel and the cuisine also has a dash of the Big Apple, as well as French and Belgian influences. Typical dishes on owner-chef Thomas Barker's menu are fillet steak topped with duck's liver and thyme crust served on truffle cream, and the rocky road hotpot (toasted marshmallows with a chocolate sauce) is a worthy indulgence. A splendid wine list numbers roughly 100 labels, mostly Cape wines but also some Argentine, Spanish and French. The expansive dining area is cosied up with clubby retro furniture, dim lighting and colourful antiques. Located in Sandton, just a couple of streets from the city's financial hub, this spot is favoured by heavyweights from nearby corporate HQs. *140 11th Street, T 011 784 1575, www.thomasmaxwell.co.za*

Bice Ristorante

The NYC-based Bice, an Italian restaurant with a focus on traditional techniques and premium quality ingredients flown in from Italy, was one of the first haute global brands to open in Johannesburg. Located in the Southern Sun Hyde Park hotel, it joins Daruma sushi bar and a whisky and cigar bar to form an entire indoor/outdoor floor of eateries, lounges and a pool area. The sedate interior of the dining room uses a subtle scheme of wood, brown and cream. Head chef Nicolai Pareti hails from Rimini and serves up dishes like chicken saltimbocca alla Romana and succulent braised veal shank with saffron risotto. The wine list is a mix of South African and Italian labels. After your meal, grab a coveted lounger by the pool for a view over the northern suburbs, spectacular during spring when the jacaranda trees bloom.
Southern Sun Hyde Park, 1st Road,
T 011 341 8080, www.tsogosunhotels.com

Canteen

The Arts on Main complex was developed from a series of warehouses dating to 1911, transformed into artists' studios, boutiques and galleries. Canteen centres around an olive- and lemon-tree studded courtyard, often the heart of the action, and its dining area (pictured) is designed to draw in sunlight. There's a gastropub menu and an all-South African wine list.
264 Fox Street, T 011 334 5947

Turn 'n Tender

In the centre of Parktown North's retail hub, Turn 'n Tender – just like Wombles (T 011 880 2470) a few doors down – is where local folk head for some serious meat. But unlike the traditional Wombles, this carnivore's heaven pays homage to contemporary decor. The space is all dark wood and cool lighting, and has an open kitchen. The brand, which now boasts five venues in Johannesburg, has been serving hefty, well-priced cuts since 1977. The steaks, basted with herbs, olive oil or a signature spice mix, are meltingly tender, although the real stars are the spare ribs (only served at the Parktown North branch). Even the 'not so full portion' is big enough for sharing; a regular order will leave you sated for a week.
Parktown Quarter, 3rd Avenue/7th Avenue, T 011 788 7933, www.turnntender.co.za

Orient

The design darling of Melrose Arch, the pan-Asian Orient is set across multiple levels, with swooping copper surfaces and chandeliers, conceived along a yin and yang theme by Anton de Kock. The menu is as sprawling as the restaurant, covering cuisines from India eastward, via its sushi and sashimi, Thai stir-fries, Chinese dim sum and Vietnamese noodles. We enjoyed the spicy prawn tom-yum soup, *sukiyaki* hotpot and crispy vegetable tempura. If you're not feeling hungry, the lower-level bar is a good place for an early evening drink and a truly mixed crowd. The wine list is heavy on South African labels. Don't leave without checking out the (OTT) bathrooms. It's very noughties, but still hip for the southern hemisphere.
4 The High Street, Melrose Arch, T 011 684 1616, www.thai-africa.co.za/orient

The Troyeville Hotel

During the 1970s, Mozambicans fleeing the civil war in Maputo settled in the Troyeville area. Subsequently, this 1939 hotel became a centre of gravity. It still delivers some of the best Mozambican-inspired Portuguese food in South Africa. You don't come here for the decor, with its kitschy mural of pink flamingoes, but be prepared to enjoy one of the city's more memorable meals. House specialities include prawns with chickpeas and heaps of green chilli salsa; fresh line fish and grilled chicken are also steeped in it. The back room often hosts dinners with major literary figures and occasional live music (check the website and book ahead). In summer, the covered patio of the hotel's Esplanada restaurant is a popular spot for a lazy Sunday lunch.
1403 Albertina Sisulu Road, T 011 402 7709, www.troyevillehotel.co.za

Tashas

Part of a small chain of modish, upscale cafés, Tashas in Atholl Square Shopping Centre brings some warmth and style to this mini-mall. The seven Johannesburg branches all have a similar earth-toned palette; marble, terrazzo and stucco are key elements, and most of the furniture is sourced from Spain and Italy. The woodwork is the result of a collaboration between owner Natasha Sideris and a South African carpenter. The modern café-style fare focuses on patisserie and Mediterranean-inspired bites, including pitta sandwiches (a tribute to the Sideris' Greek heritage). Tashas Le Parc (T 011 325 5008) in Hyde Park Corner takes it up a notch with champagne and oysters.
Shop 16, Atholl Square Shopping Centre, Katherine Street/Wierda Road East, T 011 884 0365, www.tashas.co.za

Warm & Glad

In the hipster heart of Hyde Park, this chic warehouse space, with concrete flooring, rugs, wooden furniture and green-and-gold signage, calls itself a food and wine bar. There are two on-site shops – RAD Gear & Goods, and the RAD Gallery & Bookshop, which stocks a fine collection of architecture, art, design and fashion titles. Also on sale here are limited-edition prints, mostly graphic and street art, as well as the vinyl that gets played on the decks. The volume is turned up during the afternoon, but it makes little impact on the MacBook brigade, who, utilising plentiful counter space, plug points and coffee, make this their mobile office. The no-fuss menu covers breakfast, lunch and small plates, using local ingredients. Drinks include a selection of whisky, and wines from family-owned vineyards.
357 Jan Smuts Avenue/St Alban's Road, T 011 781 0455, www.thebeachhead.co.za

ADVANCED STYLE
FRAGILE

INSIDER'S GUIDE

MILISUTHANDO BONGELA, WRITER/FASHION CONSULTANT

Nobody 'ends up' in Joburg, says Milisuthando Bongela. 'They all choose to be here. Its beauty is the people.' The city lured Bongela from the Eastern Cape, and she works as a blogger, journalist and fashion consultant. During the week she often sets up office at Warm & Glad (see p060) for the food, coffee and music, and when she's not working, she'll indulge in some retail therapy, browsing Ella Buter's avant-garde fashion at Superella (7th Avenue/9th Street, T 082 845 5551), and ready-to-wear pieces at Black Coffee (see p078) and The Space (Shop GF07, The Zone @ Rosebank, 177 Oxford Road, T 011 327 3640). Her lunchtime pick is Three Mary's (T 011 482 8618) at 44 Stanley, where 'dishes are made with love'.

At the weekend, Bongela meets friends at Kitchener's Carvery Bar (71 Juta Street, T 079 266 5077), an English-style boozer that puts on live DJs, or has cocktails in the Victoriana setting of The Winston (see p016). She loves the views from Zietsies (1 Beverley Avenue, T 082 774 4902) in actress Elzabé Zietsman's guesthouse, and also suggests dining at The Great Eastern Food Bar (see p048) or The Troyeville Hotel (see p058). After-hours, she heads to the quirky Zebra Inn (252 Albertina Sisulu Street), where one never knows quite what to expect. And she adds that everyone should spend a day in Soweto, where 'the food, people-watching and the pageantry on Vilakazi Street are a feast for eyes and stomachs'.

For full addresses, see Resources.

ARCHITOUR

A GUIDE TO JOHANNESBURG'S ICONIC BUILDINGS

Sometimes displaying a Dubai-like appreciation for the grandiose and the new, architecture in this city lacks the small-scale charm of, say, Cape Town, or the colonial elegance of African capitals like Maputo. In a landscape pockmarked with the city's mining origins, the scars of segregation are still clearly visible – whites settled into unimaginative suburban homes, and everyone else was (often forcibly) relocated to 'matchbox' houses in outlying areas. Rare examples of Johannesburg's early grand designs can be found in suburbs like Parktown (the closest thing to a Joburg vernacular is the stonework of British architect Sir Herbert Baker) and in the few remaining art deco blocks, such as the ziggurat of the 1937 Anstey's (59 Joubert Street), designed by Emley & Williamson. Meanwhile, Africa's largest concentration of high-rises came to dominate the skyline, fuelled by 1960s and 1970s gold booms.

Post-millennium, developers became aware of the architectural legacy. It's still not uncommon for heritage sites to be razed, but there are sensitive redevelopments like Turbine Hall (opposite). Large-scale works, such as StudioMAS' 2005 Walter Sisulu Square (Klipspruit Valley Road), which marks the 1955 Freedom Charter with its conical tower monument; the Soweto Theatre (see p032); and the much-loved Soccer City (see p090), are signs of a design culture that references the past, but is built to inspire and to last.
For full addresses, see Resources.

Turbine Hall

The largest of Joburg's three steam-driven power stations was constructed from 1927 to 1934. Decommissioned in 1961, it was put on standby for another decade, but with Newtown's decline, this brick monster was abandoned to squatters, most of its windows shattered. A five-year overhaul saw it transformed into the HQ of a global gold-mining firm and a conference centre by architects TPS, superbly integrating the industrial heritage with new offices, and creating design features from turbines and coal hoppers. Artworks composed of found objects discovered during the demolition of the North Boiler House complement sculptor Marco Cianfanelli's *37 Years of Gold*, a metal graph depicting fluctuating gold prices. The Forum Company (T 011 492 3888) hosts dinners once a month.
65 Ntemi Piliso Street, T 011 492 3888

Ponte City
This 173m brutalist cylinder, finished in 1975, remains Africa's tallest residential tower. Manfred Hermer Grosskopff & Lombart devised the hollow core to allow light into the inner rooms, but after its rich white residents fled post-apartheid, it became a huge rubbish dump. Ponte City has since been refurbished, its 467 flats now home to a vibrant African mix.
1 Lily Avenue

FREEDOM

Apartheid Museum

The unusual placement of this powerful museum, between an amusement park and a casino some 8km outside the city centre, does nothing to detract from its captivating exhibition space and visually arresting design by local architectural and urban planning practice GAPP. The building is crafted almost entirely from sand- and adobe-coloured stone and brick, the exterior punctuated by seven large pillars, each symbolising a tenet on which the present South African constitution is based. Inside is a series of chambers, consisting of tiny cells, lofty halls and silos, in which grey concrete floors and walls are topped by smallish windows that enhance the museum's narrative of apartheid told through photographs, documents, dioramas and numerous multimedia installations. *Northern Parkway/Gold Reef Road, T 011 309 4700, www.apartheidmuseum.org*

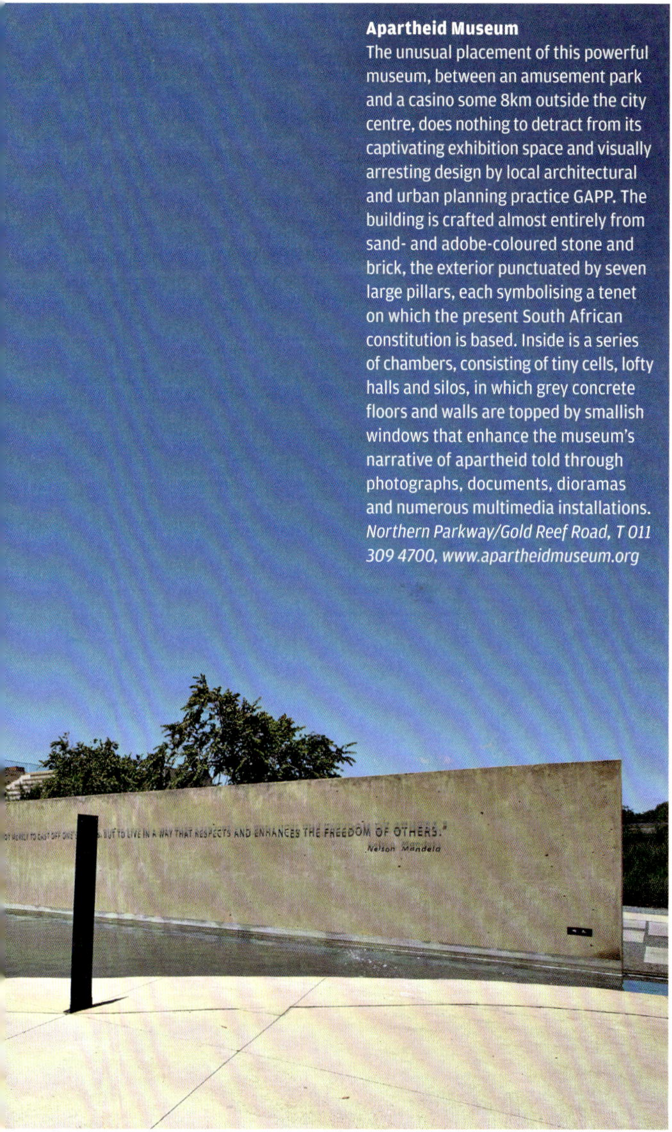

Constitutional Court

Following the shift to democratic rule, this building was the result of the first major architecture competition in South Africa, overseen by Charles Correa. The commission was won by a partnership comprising Janina Masojada and Andrew Makin from Durban with Johannesburg-based Paul Wygers, who conceived an inspiring structure inaugurated in 2004. Imposing carved wooden doors lead to a foyer incorporating more than 500 stained-glass windows and mosaic elements that reflect the traditional seating pattern of village elders. An immense collection of contemporary art is also on display. The site is adjacent to what was the country's most notorious prison complex, also open to the public.
1 Hospital Street, Constitution Hill, T 011 359 7400, www.constitutionalcourt.org.za

SHOPPING

THE BEST RETAIL THERAPY AND WHAT TO BUY

A city whose love affair with malls reaches a US intensity, Joburg may seem to lack retail edge. Yet Hyde Park Corner (see p082), Sandton City and Melrose Arch (see p084) are ahead of the game and there's style to be found amid the bland brands. For genteel high-street shopping, head to Parkhurst's 4th Avenue – highlights are the quirky jewellery at Tinsel (Shop 4, No 25, T 011 447 2761), and the covetable perspex, paper and wood wares at Green Grass (Shop 3, No 34, T 011 447 8570) – as well as cafés and restaurants.

Retail complexes are becoming more intimate and imaginative. The Bamboo Centre (see p078) is a low-intensity hangout, and the redeveloped 1930s warehouses at 44 Stanley (T 011 482 4444) house Anatomy (opposite), Lunar (T 011 726 5558), for modern knitwear, and Gallery AOP (T 011 726 2234). Maboneng's inventive destinations include Maverick Corner (300 Commissioner Street), where you'll find Stitch & Steel's wax-print clothing and Cocobelle Desserts served out of a truck; and pop-up boutiques in shipping containers at Main Street Bizarre (263 Main Street). The Sunday Market on Main at Arts on Main (see p054) is best for vintage finds.

Joburg's most worthwhile investment is contemporary art, as it's still temptingly affordable. Galleries such as David Krut (see p085), Momo (52 7th Avenue, T 011 327 3247) and Stevenson (62 Juta Street, T 011 403 1055) are just a few of the places to start.

For full addresses, see Resources.

Anatomy Design

The accomplished interior designs and custom-made furniture and fittings by Andrea Kleinloog and Megan Hesse are the focal point of some of Joburg's most attractive dining and retail spots, from Tashas Le Parc (see p059) to hip fashion label Loin Cloth & Ashes (T 072 143 2312). Source the elegantly functional furniture, lighting, kitchen- and homewares at their Anatomy showroom, an airy monochrome space done out in whitewashed brick, black floorboards and a high beamed roof. Many pieces, including the freestanding 'Lab' light, are finished in gleaming copper and brass. The store also carries work by other local designers, such as Mia Widlake's ceramics and textiles, and typographical pieces from The Letterpress Company.
44 Stanley Avenue, T 011 024 3727, www.anatomydesign.co.za

Pierre Cronje

This temple to woodwork is housed in an old bank (the safe doors are visible), where installations of work benches and tools, and a gallery of legs (opposite), illustrate the carpenter's craft. Using solid woods from sustainable forests, Cronje shows an intuitive grasp of contour, cut and grain; his skills are evident in the clever joins and the balanced lines of South African staples such as the leather-laced *riempie* tables and chairs. Handmade, refined and beautifully finished furniture and cabinets are created in signature styles like Cape Country, based on the designs of Dutch settlers, and the austere contemporary range, which incorporates a table inspired by the Bloukrans Bridge. The cheeseboard might be simpler to transport home.
Desmond Street/Kramer Road,
T 011 262 4514, www.pierrecronje.co.za

Ceramic Factory

This is an emporium of South African kitsch and nostalgia, reclaimed and cast in fine but sturdy ceramic moulds. Owner Rial Visagie finds inspiration in everything from treasured toys to milk cans from the family farm. His resulting decorative and utilitarian collections range from pastel-hued retro robots to miniature dinosaurs, doe-faced buck, cow skulls and impala-motif tiles, and each piece is individually cast, dip-glazed and then fired. You will be tempted to find room in your suitcase for the binoculars salt-and-pepper pots, an art deco-style clock or a jelly-mould lampshade. The often tongue-in-cheek pieces are beautifully set on handmade recycled wood shelving and display devices by local company Woodlady.
59 4th Avenue, Linden, T 011 057 4314, www.ceramicfactory.co.za

Drum

Inaugurated in 1951, *Drum* magazine was owned and managed by the South African multimillionaire Jim Bailey from 1951 until 1984, and is widely considered to be one of the most important magazines of the post-colonial era. It served as a showcase for influential young black writers and thinkers, like Can Themba, Nat Nakasa and even the magazine's telephonist, David Sibeko, who went on to be a key figure in the Pan Africanist Congress. Photojournalists, including Alf Kumalo, Ernest Cole and Bob Gosani, took now-iconic images of key events, from police brutality on the streets of Johannesburg to shots of the independence movement in Mozambique. The Bailey Seippel Gallery (T 071 227 0910) at Arts on Main holds an archive and sells *Drum* memorabilia, like posters and limited-edition photographs.

Black Coffee
Jacques van der Watt's breakthrough collection was a sculptural reference to head-to-toe ochres worn by Namibia's nomadic Himba. His eclectic designs also include graphic pieces inspired by electric bikes. Van der Watt's shop sells Love Jozi T-shirts too, and there's another branch in Arts on Main (T 011 334 0171).
Bamboo Centre, 53 Rustenburg Road/ 9th Street, T 011 482 9148

Kim Sacks Gallery

This boutique-like showroom is Joburg's best bet for fine-quality African crafts and artefacts, with a focus on handmade pottery. A one-time private home close to the city's gallery district on Jan Smuts Avenue, the white-walled space features pine-wood and black-cement floors (emulating traditional Zulu beer vessels). Owner Kim Sacks initially lures you with her textile pieces (from Congo or Mali) or intricately woven Zulu wirework. But it is the ceramics that set this store apart. They are thrown by artists from across South Africa, whom Sacks sources and often exclusively represents. A creative nomad who's made her own pottery since the age of 12, Sacks trained at The School of Design in Copenhagen. These are serious and collection-worthy pieces, with the price tags to match.

153 Jan Smuts Avenue, T 011 447 5804, www.kimsacksgallery.com

Life

If the products at design and architecture practice Life feel familiar, that's because you've probably come across them before in venues such as Tashas (see p059) or at upscale safari resorts. Set in Hyde Park Corner, Life's retail HQ doubles up as a restaurant and a sushi, champagne and cocktail bar that showcases its tableware. Maira Koutsoudakis' designs reveal African influence in the woven baskets, wooden stools and chairs, objets d'art and vessels, like the 'Wodaabe' pieces (above), from R2,200, made from jacaranda or poplar. The eclectic collection is augmented by global brands such as Astier de Villatte, Ortigia and DayNa Decker. Items range from ceramic plates and ornaments to glassware and pewter jugs.
Jan Smuts Avenue/William Nicol Drive,
T 011 325 4350, www.lifeinteriordesign.com

Augustine

The message on the mirror says it all: 'You look good in that.' Astroturf-covered steps, wood floors, a monochromatic scheme, an impeccably detailed ceiling and a charming garden welcome you into this townhouse conversion. Justine Coetzer and Marea Lewis offer a tailoring service specialising in out-of-the-ordinary men's suits with attention to eccentric details – material, lining, trims and buttons are all bespoke, and clients are measured in a masculine space where a metallic hunting trophy hangs over a fireplace. It takes from four to six weeks for a suit to be made, but the label also produces ready-to-wear based on contemporary trends. Highlights on our visit included biker jackets and quilted bombers in a range of fabrics and finishes. *87 6th Street, T 011 447 1566, www.augustineclothing.co.za*

Suzaan Heyns

Situated in Melrose Arch mall among the sedate chain stores, fashion designer Suzaan Heyns' boutique is an unexpected slice of avant garde – its interior a gothic Midsummer Night's Dream with a concrete woodland chandelier, reindeer heads on mannequins and a 'melting' table topped with golden skulls. Heyns is a master of graphic and architectural shapes, which she delivers with a signature feminine silhouette, using sculptural elements such as pleating and bias cuts. To accompany the collections that are often presented at South Africa Fashion Week, she creates a dramatic range of limited-edition but well-priced accessories that include statement pieces such as a concrete bowtie or giant laser-cut brass neckpieces.
Store HL53, Melrose Arch, T 011 684 1899, www.suzaanheyns.com

David Krut Bookstore

Taking in satellite locations in Cape Town and New York, David Krut oversees a mini empire. This includes a gallery (overleaf; T 011 447 0627) that presents his roster of established and emerging South Africans, from William Kentridge to Senzo Shabangu, Stephen Hobbs, Deborah Bell and Diane Victor, and two art-and-design bookstores selling his and master printer Jillian Ross' collaborations with key local artists (the second shop is in Arts on Main; T 011 334 1209). In Parkwood, facing each other across the busy Jan Smuts Avenue, is the display space, set in an old residential block, and, behind the vivid blue wall of Mexican artefact store Hadeda, the print workshop and bookstore, which carries Krut's essential monographs.
151 Jan Smuts Avenue, T 011 880 5646, www.davidkrut.com

David Krut Projects

SPORTS AND SPAS

WORK OUT, CHILL OUT OR JUST WATCH

South Africa is a sport-loving nation and Joburg is no exception. The city boasts some 2,000 parks, and throngs of runners train on the roads for the next fixture in the region's busy distance calendar. A growing number of cyclists jostle them for space, boosted by the 2013 success of Daryl Impey, the first South African to wear the *maillot jaune*, and Tour de France winner Chris Froome, who was educated here. Every month Critical Mass (jhb.criticalmass.co.za) hosts group rides, and Hunter Cycling (www.huntercycling.com) organises the Jozi Hustle night race. Virgin Active is the top gym chain, and its premium Alice Lane property (Fredman Drive, T 011 783 8410) is so state of the art, you can Skype on the treadmill.

Johannesburg takes spectator sports seriously, and has world-class rugby, cricket and football venues. The FNB Stadium (see p090) is Africa's largest – try to catch a derby between Orlando Pirates and Kaizer Chiefs. Rugby is also a massive deal, and games are held in spring and summer at Ellis Park (Currey Street/Staib Street, T 011 402 8644). Cricket, too, is a South African birthright and Test matches are played at the Wanderers (see p094).

Spa culture is starting to take hold and Africology, which uses signature products made from indigenous ingredients, is a treat; head to the Parkhurst branch (33 4th Avenue, T 011 880 0233). For lavish pampering, the Saxon Spa (opposite) is the best in town.

For full addresses, see Resources.

Saxon Spa and Studio

The spa at the Saxon (see p023) is – much like the hotel itself – the most serene and elegant in Johannesburg. Decorated with a modern-African aesthetic designed to evoke fire and water, via sandstone walls and maplewood floors, the 808 sq m spa has various chillout zones and numerous treatments on offer. The Signature Sound Therapy, for instance, induces relaxation via gongs, cymbals, singing bowls and bells. Steam rooms, plunge pools, a Rasul chamber and a hydro-capsule for baths and body wraps cap off the menu, making this a place to while more than a few hours away. There's a juice bar and café, and an outdoor heated pool (above) overlooking a wooded grove. The spa is open to non-guests who book in for a treatment.
36 Saxon Road, T 011 292 6000,
www.saxon.co.za

FNB Stadium

The renovated FNB Stadium, also known as Soccer City, hosted the FIFA World Cup opening and closing ceremonies in 2010, and is as symbolic as Herzog & de Meuron's 'bird's nest' Olympic stadium in Beijing. Located 30 minutes south-west of Joburg on the edge of Soweto, it was originally built in 1987. Boogertman + Partners designed the new structure, inspired by African pottery – its mosaic-like facade evokes an earthenware clay pot; a ring of lights at its base mimics a cooking fire. Seating 94,000, it is the largest venue of its kind in Africa. Inside, all fans have a great view, with no spectator more than 80m away from the action. The arena also staged Mandela's welcome home rally in 1990 and his memorial service in 2013.
Nasrec Road, T 011 247 5300,
www.stadiummanagement.co.za

Wyatt Hairdressing and Barbering

When Candice Wyatt-Minter renovated her salon in 2013, she commissioned Dokter and Misses (see p026) to create an interior that would represent her commitment to sustainability, and provide a welcoming ambience based around green principles. Custom solutions in the voluminous space include suspended double-sided mirrors, compact swivel tables and a flattering lighting plan featuring LEDs and pieces from Dokter and Misses' 'Conduit' range. The diamond-grinded concrete floor and powder-coated steel is offset by a series of living green installations by Joe Paine, which, along with the mesh-and-felt sofa seating by Ronel Jordaan, conveys a sense of levity. Wyatt stocks eco-friendly hair products made by Italian company Davines.
44 Stanley Avenue, T 011 482 6111,
www.wyatthairdressing.com

Wanderers Stadium

Located in the northern suburb of Illovo, the 34,000-seat Wanderers is the city's top cricket stadium and the largest Test venue in the country. Opened in 1956, it was formerly a bastion of the old-school, white South African elite. The ground was given a big overhaul in the early 1990s when South Africa was admitted back into the global cricket community following the end of apartheid. Today, it can operate day and night thanks to huge floodlights towering 65m over the pitch. Home to the Bizhub Highveld Lions team, Wanderers is widely considered the best cricket facility in Africa and includes 182 private suites for deep-pocketed fans. Evening bish-bash-bosh games of T20 are great fun and only last a few hours. Next door is Wanderers Golf Club (T 011 447 3311), regularly rated one of the top 10 courses in South Africa.
Corlett Drive, T 011 340 1500,
www.wanderers.co.za

ESCAPES

WHERE TO GO IF YOU WANT TO LEAVE TOWN

It's a popular local joke that when urbanites want to escape for the weekend, they fly to Cape Town. Just over two hours away (and served by a clutch of low-cost airlines), its mix of beach, retail and quality cuisine can't be beat. But it is not your only option. Armed with an Africa Airpass from Star Alliance (www.staralliance.com), a hire car or even a bus ticket, all southern Africa is within reach.

The most logical getaway has to be the interior. KwaZulu-Natal province, which is the closest wildlife haven with access to the 'big five' – elephants, buffalo, lions, leopards and rhino – is served by operators like &Beyond (T 011 809 4300, www.andbeyond.com), which runs the secluded Phinda Private Game Reserve. Further afield, the intimate Molori Safari Lodge (T 014 778 8000) offers more of a luxurious experience, while Great Plains Conservation (www.greatplainsconservation.com) manages camps in Botswana, Kenya and Tanzania focusing on the environment and community development. And you shouldn't forget that Mozambique is just next door. The capital, Maputo (opposite), connects visitors to the pristine beaches further north near Pemba and Vilanculos.

Much closer to Joburg, the Cradle of Humankind (see p098), a UNESCO World Heritage Site, is a beautiful rural retreat. It's home to many of the world's oldest human fossils, the Nirox Foundation sculpture park and one of the finest restaurants in South Africa.
For full addresses, see Resources.

Maputo, Mozambique

The recent tourism boom in Mozambique has centred around Inhambane, Xai Xai and Vilanculos, but its oceanfront capital is still compelling. An hour from Joburg by plane, this once war-torn city is now a hip weekend getaway. It's been 40 years since the Portuguese left but much of the tropical modernist architecture remains, including Nuno Craveiro Lopes' 1962 Igreja de Santo António da Polana (above; T +258 2149 1197), along with ornate structures such as the art deco cathedral. The Polana Serena Hotel (T +258 2124 1700), designed by Herbert Baker in 1922, has undergone a lavish makeover. Take Maputo's pulse at the Centre Culturel Franco Mozambicain (T +258 2131 4590) – the Victorian building now has a gallery and music venues – and try the prawns at Piri Piri (T +258 2149 2379) and Zambi (T +258 843 392 624).

Cradle of Humankind

An hour's drive from Joburg, the Cradle of Humankind is unique, combining ancient history with contemporary art and cuisine. Many remains of human ancestors have been found here – get an insight at the Maropeng visitors' centre (T 014 577 9000) and Sterkfontein Caves. Stay in one of the 14 suites at the Forum Homini hotel (T 011 668 7000). Its interiors feature stone walls, exposed beams and African fabrics, and the restaurant, Roots, has built a fine reputation. A short drive away is another culinary gem, Le Sel @ The Cradle (right; Route T9, Kromdraai Road), run by chef Brouphy Mathe. Near a valley of grassland and dolomite ridges, it offers seasonal dishes in a stylish, pared-down setting. The nearby Nirox foundation (T 082 854 6963; appointment only) is also a must-visit, an exquisite wooded landscape interspersed with lakes and studded with contemporary South African sculpture.

Freedom Park, Pretoria

Set on a ridge overlooking Pretoria, about 40 minutes north of Joburg, Freedom Park is a memorial marking South Africa's long struggle for democracy. The 52-hectare site was conceived by former president Thabo Mbeki and opened in 2007. Another project led by Joburg firm GAPP, working with architects MRA and MMA, the park includes a place of remembrance (above) with an eternal flame, water features and an amphitheatre for state events. Evoking architecture from all over Africa, the main structures are linked by spiral paths, made from Phalaborwa quartzite rock. The Wall of Names is an impressive 697m long, and commemorates those who gave their lives in the defining conflicts of the country's history. Set aside two hours for a full tour. *De Koch Street/3rd Avenue, T 012 336 4000, www.freedompark.co.za*

Mapungubwe Interpretation Centre

Architects Peter Rich designed this superb tribute to the old kingdom of Mapungubwe, a gold- and ivory-trading civilisation that flourished in the 13th and 14th centuries. The 1,500 sq m visitors centre (above) sits on a slope amid sandstone formations, mopane woodlands, riverine forest and baobab trees. To create the stone-clad vaults that house the historic artefacts at this World Heritage Site, the architects referenced a 700-year-old construction system. Mapungubwe Park borders both Botswana and Zimbabwe and is included within the Limpopo-Shashe Transfrontier Conservation Area. As well as the big five, keep your eyes peeled for hyena, antelope and 400 species of birds. It's a six-hour drive up the N1 out of Johannesburg.
Near Musina, Vhembe, Limpopo,
T 015 534 7923, www.sanparks.org

Singita Sweni Lodge, Kruger
On the Mozambican border, flanked by the Sweni River within Kruger National Park, are six stilted glass and dark wood suites designed by Boyd Ferguson. The lodge has extraordinary wildlife views from decks nestled in the trees, and it serves excellent African fusion cuisine. Satara is a 90-minute flight from Joburg.
Kruger National Park, near Satara,
T 013 735 5500, www.singita.com

NOTES

SKETCHES AND MEMOS

RESOURCES

CITY GUIDE DIRECTORY

A

&Beyond 096
T 011 809 4300
www.andbeyond.com

Africology 088
33 4th Avenue
T 011 880 0233
www.africologyspa.com

Alexander Forbes Building 010
115 West Street
T 011 269 0000

Anatomy Design 073
44 Stanley
44 Stanley Avenue
T 011 024 3727
www.anatomydesign.co.za

Anstey's 064
59 Joubert Street

Apartheid Museum 068
Northern Parkway/Gold Reef Road
T 011 309 4700
www.apartheidmuseum.org

Artisan Lofts 031
264 Market Street

Arts on Main 054
264 Fox Street
T 011 334 1054
www.mabonengprecinct.com

Assaggi 046
Post Office Centre
30 Rudd Road
T 011 268 1370
www.assaggi.co.za

Augustine 083
87 6th Street
T 011 447 1566
www.augustineclothing.co.za

B

Bailey Seippel Gallery 077
Arts on Main
264 Fox Street
T 071 227 0910

Bamboo Centre 079
53 Rustenburg Road/9th Street
T 011 726 1701
www.bamboo-online.co.za

Barbican 009
Loveday Street/President Street

Bice Ristorante 052
Southern Sun Hyde Park
1st Road
T 011 341 8080
www.tsogosunhotels.com

Black Coffee 078
Bamboo Centre
53 Rustenburg Road/9th Street
T 011 482 9148
Arts on Main
264 Fox Street
T 011 334 0171
www.blackcoffee.co.za

The Blackanese 040
20 Kruger Street
T 011 024 9455
www.theblackanese.co.za

C

Canteen 054
Arts on Main
264 Fox Street
T 011 334 5947
www.mabonengprecinct.com

Carlton Centre 013
150 Commissioner Street
T 011 308 1331

F

44 Stanley 072
44 Stanley Avenue
T 011 482 4444
www.44stanley.co.za

The Fashion Kapitol 024
103 Pritchard Street
T 011 333 7372

Father Coffee 041
Shop 2
73 Juta Street
T 082 513 4258
www.fathercoffee.co.za

FNB Stadium 090
Nasrec Road
T 011 247 5300
www.stadiummanagement.co.za

The Forum Company 065
T 011 492 3888
www.theforum.co.za

Freedom Park 100
De Koch Street/3rd Avenue
Pretoria
T 012 336 4000
www.freedompark.co.za

G

Gallery AOP 072
44 Stanley
44 Stanley Avenue
T 011 726 2234
www.galleryaop.com

The Good Luck Club 041
3 Corlett Drive
T 011 447 3816
www.thegoodluckclub.co.za

Goodman Gallery 035
163 Jan Smuts Avenue
T 011 788 1113
www.goodman-gallery.com

Great Dane 038
5 De Beer Street
T 011 403 1136

The Great Eastern Food Bar 048
Bamboo Centre
53 Rustenberg Road/9th Street
T 011 482 2910

Green Grass 072
Shop 3
34 4th Avenue
T 011 447 8570
www.greengrassdesign.co.za

The Grillhouse 040
Shop 70
The Firs
Oxford Road/Biermann Avenue
T 011 880 3945
www.thegrillhouse.co.za

H

Hector Pieterson Museum 032
8287 Khumalo Street
Orlando West
T 011 536 0611

Hillbrow Tower 012
Goldreich Street/Banket Street

I

Igreja de Santo António da Polana 097
Avenida Armando Tivane
Maputo
Mozambique
T +258 2149 1197

K

Kim Sacks Gallery 080
153 Jan Smuts Avenue
T 011 447 5804
www.kimsacksgallery.com

Sentech Tower 009
Symons Road
Service Station 048
Bamboo Centre
53 Rustenberg Road/9th Street
T 011 726 1701
Soweto Outdoor Adventures 024
Dynamo Street
T 072 692 8159
Soweto Theatre 033
Bolani Road/Bolani Link Road
Soweto
T 011 930 7461
www.sowetotheatre.org.za
The Space 062
Shop GF07
The Zone @ Rosebank
177 Oxford Road
T 011 327 3640
www.thezoneatrosebank.co.za
Stanley Beer Yard 044
44 Stanley
44 Stanley Avenue
T 011 482 5791
Stevenson 072
62 Juta Street
T 011 403 1055
www.stevenson.info
Superella 062
7th Avenue/9th Street
T 082 845 5551
Suzaan Heyns 084
Store HL53
Melrose Arch
T 011 684 1899
www.suzaanheyns.com

T

Tashas 059
Shop 16
Atholl Square Shopping Centre
Katherine Street/Wierda Road East
T 011 884 0365
www.tashas.co.za
Tashas Le Parc 059
Shop 29
William Nicol Drive/Jan Smuts Avenue
Hyde Park
T 011 325 5008
www.tashas.co.za
Thomas Maxwell 051
140 11th Street
T 011 784 1575
www.thomasmaxwell.co.za
Three Mary's 062
44 Stanley
44 Stanley Avenue
T 011 482 8618
www.threemarys.co.za
Tinsel 072
Shop 4
25 4th Avenue
T 011 447 2761
www.tinsel.co.za
The Troyeville Hotel 058
1403 Albertina Sisulu Road
T 011 402 7709
www.troyevillehotel.co.za
Turbine Hall 065
65 Ntemi Piliso Street
T 011 492 3888
Turn 'n Tender 056
Parktown Quarter
3rd Avenue/7th Avenue
T 011 788 7933
www.turnntender.co.za

HOTELS

ADDRESSES AND ROOM RATES

African Pride Melrose Arch Hotel 022
Room rates:
double, from R2,570;
Superior Room, from R2,940
1 Melrose Square
Melrose Arch
T 011 214 6666
www.africanpridehotels.com

AtholPlace 016
Room rates:
double, from R4,800
90 Pretoria Avenue
T 011 783 3410
www.atholplace.co.za

The Bannister 016
Room rates:
double, from R495
9 De Beer Street
T 011 403 6888
www.bannisterhotel.co.za

Forum Homini 098
Room rates:
double, from R3,500
Letamo Game Estate
Bartlet Road
Kromdraai
Mogale City
T 011 668 7000
www.forumhomini.com

The Hamilton 020
Room rates:
double, from R1,450;
Suite 4, from R1,650
28 Grosvenor Avenue
T 011 447 9280
www.thehamilton.co.za

InterContinental 016
Room rates:
double, R3,250
Maude Street/5th Street
T 011 780 5555
www.ihg.com

The Maslow 016
Room rates:
double, from R3,180
146 Rivonia Road
T 010 226 4600
www.suninternational.com/maslow

Molori Safari Lodge 096
Room rates:
double, from R10,250
Madikwe Game Reserve
North West Province
T 014 778 8000
www.molorisafari.com

Monarch 016
Room rates:
double, from R2,750
167 Oxford Road
T 011 341 2000
www.monarchhotel.co.za

The Peech 017
Room rates:
double, from R2,400;
Garden Suite, from R2,800
61 North Street
T 011 537 9797
www.thepeech.co.za

Polana Serena Hotel 097
Room rates:
double, R4,170
1380 Avenida Julius Nyerere
Maputo
Mozambique
T +258 2124 1700
www.serenahotels.com

Radisson Blu Gautrain 016
Room rates:
double, R1,250
Rivonia Road
T 011 286 1000
www.radissonblu.com

The Satyagraha House 018
Room rates:
double, R1,735;
Henri Polak Superior Room, from R2,960;
Cottage, from R4,850
15 Pine Road
T 011 485 5928
www.satyagrahahouse.com

Saxon Hotel, Villas and Spa 023
Room rates:
double, from R4,950;
Executive Luxury Suite, R6,500;
Luxury One Bedroom, from R9,900
36 Saxon Road
T 011 292 6000
www.saxon.co.za

Singita Sweni Lodge 102
Room rates:
Standard Double, from R29,200
Kruger National Park
Near Satara
T 013 735 5500
www.singita.com

12 Decades 021
Room rates:
double, R870
Main Street Life Building
286 Fox Street
T 011 026 5601
www.urbanhiphotels.com/12-decades

Westcliff 016
Room rates:
double, from R4,890
67 Jan Smuts Avenue
T 011 481 6000
www.westcliff.co.za

The Winston Hotel 016
Room rates:
double, from R2,530
6 Tottenham Avenue
T 011 268 3140
www.thewinstonhotel.co.za

WALLPAPER* CITY GUIDES

Executive Editor
Rachael Moloney

Editor
Jeremy Case

Author
Laurice Taitz

Art Editor
Eriko Shimazaki
Original Design
Loran Stosskopf
Map Illustrator
Russell Bell

Photography Editor
Elisa Merlo
Assistant Photography Editor
Nabil Butt

Production Controller
Natalia Read

Chief Sub-Editor
Nick Mee
Sub-Editor
Farah Shafiq

Editorial Assistant
Emilee Jane Tombs

Contributors
Nechama Brodie
David Kaufman

Intern
Victoria Purcell

Wallpaper* ® is a registered trademark of IPC Media Limited

First published 2010
Revised and updated 2014

All prices are correct at the time of going to press, but are subject to change.

Printed in China

Phaidon Press Limited
Regent's Wharf
All Saints Street
London N1 9PA

Phaidon Press Inc
65 Bleecker Street
New York, NY 10012

Phaidon® is a registered trademark of Phaidon Press Limited

www.phaidon.com

A CIP Catalogue record for this book is available from the British Library.

ISBN 978 0 7148 6831 8

PHOTOGRAPHERS

Iwan Baan
Mapungubwe Interpretation Centre, p101

BAHA
Drum magazine, p077

Jonathan de Villiers
Ponte City, pp066-067

Alex Hill
Hillbrow Tower, p012
Carlton Centre, p013
11 Diagonal Street, pp014-015
The Peech, p017
African Pride Melrose Arch Hotel, p022
Saxon Hotel, Villas and Spa, p023
Museum of Man & Science, p030
Orlando Towers, pp032-033
CIRCA, p034
Goodman Gallery, p035
Assaggi, p046
Thomas Maxwell, p051
Bice Ristorante, pp052-053
Canteen, pp054-055
Turn 'n Tender, p056
Orient, p057
The Troyeville Hotel, p058
Apartheid Museum, pp068-069
Constitutional Court, pp070-071
Black Coffee, pp078-079
Kim Sacks Gallery, pp080-081
Saxon Spa and Studio, p089
FNB Stadium, pp090-091
Wanderers Stadium, pp094-095
Le Sel @ The Cradle, pp098-099
Freedom Park, p100

David Ross
Johannesburg city view, inside front cover
The Satyagraha House, p018, p019
The Hamilton, p020
12 Decades, p021
The Whippet in Linden, p025
Dokter and Misses, pp026-027
Wits Art Museum, p028, p029
Artisan Lofts, p031
The Winehouse, p036
The Leopard, p037
Randlords, pp038-039
Father Coffee, p041
Croft & Co, pp042-043
Stanley Beer Yard, p044, p045
Cube Tasting Kitchen, p047
The Great Eastern Food Bar, pp048-049
La Luna, p050
Warm & Glad, pp060-061
Milisuthando Bongela, p063
Turbine Hall, p065
Anatomy Design, p073
Pierre Cronje, p074, p075
Ceramic Factory, p076
Augustine, p083
Suzaan Heyns, p084
David Krut Bookstore, p085
David Krut Projects, pp086-087
Wyatt Hairdressing and Barbering, p092, p093

F Rigaud/Travel-Images
Igreja de Santo António da Polana, p097

JOHANNESBURG

A COLOUR-CODED GUIDE TO THE HOT 'HOODS

SANDTON

United by wealth, the multiracial business class of new South Africa works and plays here

BRAAMFONTEIN/NEWTOWN

These formerly dull office districts are now a haven for artists, designers and developers

THE PARKS

Abundant shops and eateries grant lush Parkhurst and its environs a metropolitan feel

MELROSE

A rare pedestrian-friendly enclave in a city geared to car travel, and a great spot to eat out

MABONENG/CBD

World-class architecture and Africa's tallest skyline sit side-by-side with inner-city decay

MELVILLE

Youthful and buzzy, this Victorian-era district is a hot zone for Johannesburg nightlife

For a full description of each neighbourhood, see the Introduction.
Featured venues are colour-coded, according to the district in which they are located.